This book is a mu: and it provokes you to want to know God and His Word in a deeper, more intimate way. Pastor Eric Fearman brings out truths from the Word of God on the power of the imagination—truths that will take you up to a new level of victorious Christian living.

—Dr. Hazel Hill, Missions Director,
Victory Churches International

I believe that if the truths in this book are understood and applied in our lives, families, and churches, a great spiritual awakening will occur. "Now to Him who is able to do exceedingly abundantly above all that we ask or think [imagine], according to the power that works in us" (Ephesians 3:20).

—Dr. George Hill, President,
Victory Churches International

IMAGINE
GOD

H. ERIC FEARMAN

CREATION
HOUSE
A STRANG COMPANY

IMAGINE GOD by H. Eric Fearman
Published by Creation House
A Strang Company
600 Rinehart Road
Lake Mary, Florida 32746
www.strangbookgroup.com

Scripture quotations marked KJV are from the King James Version of the Bible.

Scripture quotations marked NKJV are from the New King James Version of the Bible. Copyright © 1979, 1980, 1982 by Thomas Nelson, Inc., publishers. Used by permission.

Scripture quotations marked AMP are from the Amplified Bible. Old Testament copyright © 1965, 1987 by the Zondervan Corporation. The Amplified New Testament copyright © 1954, 1958, 1987 by the Lockman Foundation. Used by permission.

Scripture quotations marked THE MESSAGE are from *The Message: The Bible in Contemporary English*, copyright © 1993, 1994, 1995, 1996, 2000, 2001, 2002. Used by permission of NavPress Publishing Group.

Design Director: Bill Johnson

Cover design by Justin Evans and Nathan Morgan

Library of Congress Control Number: 2010933293
International Standard Book Number: 978-1-61638-221-6

First Edition

10 11 12 13 14 — 9 8 7 6 5 4 3 2 1
Printed in the United States of America

CONTENTS

PREFACE

OUR GOD MAKES no mistakes. He knew just what He was doing when He made you. It doesn't matter what you look like or how high your IQ is, God made you for His eternal glory, and He has a purpose for your life no matter how insignificant you think you are. We are all created in the very image of God, and we all reflect His glory and are commissioned to do His will in the Earth. We will never be able to comprehend this truth until we begin to see ourselves as God sees us. God sees us as His righteousness, His light, His children, His workmanship, His heirs, His peculiar treasures, and His victorious church.

Is this how you see yourself? In order for us to see ourselves as God sees us, we must learn to look at our lives through God's eyes. The way to see through His eyes is to see our lives through His Living Word. This is not natural for us to do because God's Word is of spiritual content, so we must learn to see spiritually—stop living by natural sight and start living according to God's Word. God has enabled us to do this by commitment to unbroken fellowship with His eternal Word within our imaginations, our spiritual eyes.

Chapter 1

THE POWER OF IMAGINATION

EVERY GOOD AND useful invention was given to us by God. From the wheel to the airplane, God put seeds of wisdom in man's heart; then man's imagination formed thoughts into ideas and plans until the invention was visible inside the mind, and became a physical reality by faith.

> I wisdom dwell with prudence, and find out knowledge of witty inventions.
> —PROVERBS 8:12, KJV

> Every good gift and every perfect gift is from above and cometh down from the Father of lights, with whom is no variableness, neither shadow of turning.
> —JAMES 1:17, KJV

I saw our church, Ambassadors for Christ, in my imagination long before I knew the hope of His calling. I saw myself preaching before I had the desire to preach. God put that seed of wisdom in my imagination, and not long after that thoughts about preaching started to form. Then a plan to go to seminary was formed because I came into agreement with the idea. It all started with a seed of wisdom being planted in my imagination. I was able to come into agreement with that word of wisdom because my mind was and still is in the renewal process. A renewed mind is able to approve that good and acceptable perfect will of God. Once I knew God's will, it was easy for me to accept because His divine will was designed perfectly for me, and the desires for that will were already placed in my heart by God. One of our major problems in Christianity today is our minds are not focused on the Living Word, and we must credit the devil for that. He is constantly creating distraction after distraction to keep our minds off the Word of truth. The mind renewal process must have preeminence in our lives so that we will know the will of God for our lives. We must know what is from God and what is from Satan. Paul is practically begging us to renew our minds with God's Holy Word. In Romans 12:1–2:

> I beseech you therefore, brethren, by the mercies of God, that ye present your bodies a living sacrifice, holy, acceptable unto God, which is your reasonable service. And be not conformed to this world: but be ye transformed by the renewing of your mind, that ye may prove what is that good, and acceptable, and perfect, will of God (KJV).

The imagination is in the deepest part of our mind or heart, and this is the place where thoughts are formed into ideas and plans. Notice that Paul uses the words *conformed* and *transformed*. Paul is telling us not to allow our thoughts to form into worldly ideas and plans, but to let God's Word transform our thinking so that we may know His good and perfect will for our lives.

The Greek translation for the English word *transformed* is *metamorphoo*, which means "to change to another form." God's Word planted in our imagination will change the way we think and, therefore, change our lives.

> For as he thinketh in his heart, so is he.
> —PROVERBS 23:7, KJV

I never thought in a million years I would be preaching and teaching God's Word, but God planted a seed of wisdom that allowed me to imagine it, and from that same seed came the faith to step out and do it. Our minds are renewed when the Word of the Lord fills our imagination. This is when old thought patterns and plans are stripped away, just like a caterpillar strips away that old form and takes on the new form of a beautiful butterfly. What we have to keep in mind is the process of renewal by the Word takes time and patience, which we all fall short of in this microwave society we live in. Look at it this way: some of us spent the majority of our lives thinking according to this fallen world system. Now you have come into the kingdom with a new set of values and priorities that many of you had never once thought about, so it's going to take some major renovation. You cannot have a renovation project by building upon the old; you must tear down old walls and old floors and replace them with new walls and new floors. But what I see happening in the church today is people trying to keep those old walls erected and adding some new ones to the old. We must understand there is spiritual warfare going on in our minds, and the things of the devil must be destroyed, not toyed with. You see, we were born in sin, which means we were born to sin, and this fallen nature is at enmity with God. It's vital that we realize God has given us His Word; this alone is an honor and a privilege. I *beseech* you, therefore, by the mercies of God, that you renew your mind daily with God's eternal Word. God's Word within our imagination will transform worldly thoughts into kingdom thoughts, which in turn will allow us to see the kingdom in operation, and when we begin to see the kingdom operate within our imagination we will experience it on Earth. Remember what Jesus told the Pharisees when they asked Him when the kingdom should come. He told them, "The kingdom of God cometh not with observation, behold the kingdom of God is within you."

> Therefore, if anyone is in Christ, he is a new
> creation; old things have passed away, behold; all
> things have become new.
> —2 Corinthians 5:17, NKJV

Think back—are there any good ideas or plans that you gave up on because you just weren't sure if they were from God? Let me suggest to you—keep your heart full of the Word. A renewed mind will know the good and acceptable perfect will of God. It's of the utmost importance in these last days. God is saying, "My people are destroyed for lack of knowledge of my will." Hebrews 4:12 tells us that God's Word is a "discerner of the thoughts and intents of the heart." The English word *discerner* is from the Greek word *kritikos*, which means "to pass judgment." God's Word judges our thoughts and intentions. It shows us whether our thoughts and plans are good or evil. God's Word dwelling richly in you will give you keen perception to know with what spirit your thoughts originate. This is so important because staying in the center of God's will brings prosperity to every area of our lives. So many Christians live unproductive lives because they're just not sure what God has for them to do. Is that you? Listen, you don't have to stay in the dark any longer—just start feeding on God's Living Word day and night and watch what happens. First you will begin to develop a positive attitude followed by a sense of belonging. God's Word is His eternal love letter to His children. Then as the Word gets deeper in your mind it reaches the imagination, your "spiritual video screen," which is where plans and ideas from God form into visual images and scenes. Inner vision from God's Word releases faith because we see ourselves doing what we didn't think was possible, but with God all things are possible.

Chapter 2

THE EVIL OF IMAGINATION

*And GOD saw that the wickedness of man was great
in the earth, and that every imagination of the
thoughts of his heart was only evil continually.*

GENESIS 6:5, KJV

GOD DESTROYED THE first world because their imaginations were evil continually. That was a civilization doomed for destruction because civilizations are first conceived in the imagination.

> When the righteous are in authority, the people rejoice; But when a wicked man rules, the people groan.
>
> —PROVERBS 29:2, NKJV

Let's look at Genesis 8:21:

> And the LORD said in his heart, I will not again curse the ground any more for man's sake; for the imagination of man's heart is evil from his youth (KJV).

This tells us mankind did not always have evil imaginations. This started in the Garden of Eden and progressively grew worse. This started when Adam and Eve ate from the tree of the knowledge of good and evil. The good knowledge they gained wasn't really good because it was gained in disobedience to the Lord God. In addition, it was separated from the tree of life, Christ Jesus. Listen to what Jesus tells us in John 15:5:

> I am the vine, you are the branches. He who abides
> in Me, and I in him, bears much fruit; for without
> Me you can do nothing (NKJV).

It's just like people who have not received salvation through Jesus Christ doing good deeds. They may be sown in the flesh and have wrong motives.

Let's take a look at this word *imagination* and see what we find. The word *imagination* comes from the Hebrew word *yet ser,* which means "to form" and "conception." Looking at this translation, it appears that the imagination is the part of our mind that forms thoughts and gives birth to our plans and ideas.

An evil imagination forms evil thoughts and gives birth to evil ideas and plans. God had to destroy the first world because the thoughts within their imaginations were evil continually. Therefore, they were only capable of producing evil ideas, evil desires, and wicked plans and dreams. But the Bible tells us Noah was a just man and perfect in his generations, and Noah walked with God. You see, God will always have a remnant people. It has always been that way as it is today. In Noah's day the imagination of man's heart was only evil continually, and this brought judgment from God by way of the flood. This shows us the power of the imagination—the place in our minds where dreams, plans, visions, and ideas are born. Children have very active imaginations, but they only imagine things they have knowledge of, and they get knowledge from what they're taught and what they see. If all they see for the most part is evil, they will imagine evil in their hearts. This creates a downward spiral and brings judgment from a holy and just God. Adam and Eve had no knowledge of evil; therefore, they were incapable of imagining evil until they ate from that forbidden tree. The first fruit that was sown in their imagination was fear. Fear came forth first from their newly gained knowledge of evil. Look at Genesis 3:8–10:

> And they heard the voice of the LORD God walking in the garden in the cool of the day: and Adam and his wife hid themselves from the presence of the LORD God amongst the trees of the garden. And the LORD God called unto Adam, and said unto him, Where art thou? And he said, I heard thy voice in the garden, and I was afraid, because I was naked; and I hid myself (KJV).

Adam and Eve experienced fear for the first time, as they were afraid of their loving Father God. Now that they had knowledge of evil, fear entered their lives. Satan is the giver of fear and torment because he exists in fear and torment. Don't be misled, Satan lives in fear, and he's terrified of the judgment coming his way soon! He is also a liar. Listen to what our Lord says about him:

> You are of your father the devil, and the desires of your father you want to do. He was a murderer from the beginning, and does not stand in the truth, because there is no truth in him. When he speaks a lie, he speaks from his own resources, for he is a liar and the father of it.
> —JOHN 8:44, NKJV

Now that knowledge of evil had entered Adam and Eve's imagination, so did fear and so did lies. The devil now had access to their imagination. When they let in knowledge of evil, they let in knowledge of Satan, fear, and demonic lies. This has been passed down to all mankind. I bet the devil lied to them by telling them to run from God's presence because God would destroy them. Thousands of years later, he's still telling mankind to run from God's presence. Remember, the word *imagination* comes from the Hebrew word that means "to form" and "conception." The devil's wicked job is to deposit lies into your imagination so that you will form thoughts that are not true and give birth to fear.

> There is no fear in love; but perfect love casteth out fear: because fear hath torment. He that feareth is not made perfect in love.
> —1 JOHN 4:18, KJV

God's job is to deposit truth into your imagination so that you will form thoughts that are true and give birth to love.

> Now hope does not disappoint, because the love of God has been poured out in our hearts by the Holy Spirit who was given to us.
> —ROMANS 5:5, NKJV

> Behold, You desire truth in the inward parts, And in the hidden part You will make me to know wisdom.
> —PSALM 51:6, NKJV

We have all inherited evil imaginations that cause us to sin against God. This happened because our parents, Adam and Eve, disobeyed God and gained the knowledge of evil. Along with evil knowledge came the evil one. You see, he has a right to what's his. Look at what Jesus says in John 14:30:

> I will no longer talk much with you, for the ruler of this world is coming, and he has nothing in Me (NKJV).

Unlike us, Satan owned nothing in our Lord's imagination, absolutely nothing. Remember, Jesus was not and is not in Adam. Therefore, Jesus was not subject to the knowledge of evil, and Satan had no claim to Him or any entry to His mind.

> For as in Adam all die, even so in Christ all shall
> be made alive.
> —1 CORINTHIANS 15:22, NKJV

But our remedy is the Word of the Living God, which cleanses our imagination and causes us to triumph in Christ Jesus.

> For the word of God is living and powerful, and
> sharper than any two-edged sword, piercing even
> to the division of soul and spirit, and of joints
> and marrow, and is a discerner of the thoughts
> and intents of the heart. And there is no creature
> hidden from His sight, but all things are naked
> and open to the eyes of Him to whom we must
> give account.
> —HEBREWS 4:12–13, NKJV

Let's look at Jeremiah 11:8, God's words toward Israel after the flood:

> Yet they obeyed not, nor inclined their ear, but
> walked every one in the imagination of their evil
> heart: therefore I will bring upon them all the
> words of this covenant, which I commanded them
> to do; but they did them not (KJV).

This text points out to us that our imagination is behind our thoughts, and it has the power to direct our hearts and therefore our actions. Our imagination is the place of conception in our mind. Let's look at Psalm 68:20:

> He that is our God is the God of salvation; and
> unto God the Lord belong the issues from death
> (kjv).

Let's also look at Proverbs 4:23:

> Keep thy heart with all diligence; for out of it are
> the issues of life (kjv).

What these two scriptures tell us is very important. The first verse tells us God is the God of deliverance, and He owns the departure from death. Notice the word *issues* is translated from the Hebrew word *totsa aha*, which means "departure." The next scripture tells us to guard our hearts or thoughts, for out of them flows departure from life. This is very serious because our thoughts can put us in the grave if we allow them to. Our imagination forms godly thoughts or demonic plans, visions, ideas, and dreams. So we are choosing life in God or death with Satan. It's just that simple.

> How can a young man cleanse his way? By taking
> heed according to Your word.
>
> —Psalm 119:9, nkjv

> Thy word have I hid in mine heart, that I might
> not sin against thee.
>
> —Psalm 119:11, kjv

> And I will walk at liberty, For I seek Your
> precepts.
>
> —Psalm 119:45, nkjv

Chapter 3

THE SANCTIFIED IMAGINATION

While we look not at the things which are seen,
but at the things which are not seen.

2 CORINTHIANS 4:18, KJV

THE ONLY WAY we're able to see things that are invisible to the physical eyes is through our spiritual eyes within our imagination. The devil has been (and still is) terrified of mankind learning the power of a sanctified imagination. A sanctified imagination has been renewed by the Word of God, and it sees us as God sees us.

- Healed

- Set free

- Prosperous

- Wise

- Victorious

- More than a conqueror

- Walking in love

- Sealed by the Holy Spirit

- Cleansed by the blood

- Full of faith

- Full of hope

- With signs, wonders, and miracles following

- Faithful witnesses

- The salt of the Earth

The devil has attached words like fairy tales, myths, make be-lieve, la-la land, and daydreamer to our imagination to discredit it and its use. Just because you can't see something with your physical eyes doesn't mean it's not real!

> For the things which are seen are temporal; but the things which are not seen are eternal.
> —2 Corinthians 4:18, kjv

So let's start this journey on the sanctified imagination.

> Sanctify them through thy truth: thy word is truth.
> —John 17:17, kjv

Jesus is praying for us, that we would be sanctified by God's Word.

> Husbands, love your wives, just as Christ also loved the church and gave Himself for her, that He might sanctify and cleanse her with the washing of water by the word.
> —Ephesians 5:25–26, nkjv

Word is the translated Greek word *logos*, which means "the ex-pression of thought." God is one with His thoughts just like we are one with our thoughts. What's closer to you than your thoughts?

When we put God's thoughts deep into our imagination, our imagination does what it's designed to do, and that's to form thoughts and give birth to new ideas, new plans, new ministries, new businesses, new churches, and so on. You see, God's thoughts are much higher than our human thoughts. God's thoughts are supernatural, and when they get deep in our imagination, supernatural ideas and plans are birthed. Things you never thought you could do are now beginning to seem possible. Now that the supernatural has been birthed, a miracle is manifesting. And as you continue to water that seed God planted in your imagination, you begin to see yourself healed regardless of the doctor's report and you begin to see yourself financially blessed regardless of your present circumstances. Then comes faith that is evidence of something not seen, and according to your faith it shall be done unto you. All of this happens because God's supernatural Word abides deep in your imagination.

> Cease not to give thanks for you, making mention of you in my prayers; That the God of our Lord Jesus Christ, the Father of glory, may give unto you the spirit of wisdom and revelation in the knowledge of him: The *eyes of your understanding* being enlightened; that ye may know what is the hope of his calling, and what the riches of the glory of his inheritance in the saints
> —EPHESIANS 1:16–18, KJV, EMPHASIS ADDED

> [For I always pray to] the God of our Lord Jesus Christ, the Father of glory, that He may grant you a spirit of wisdom and revelation [of insight into mysteries and secrets] in the [deep and intimate] knowledge of Him. *By having the eyes of your heart* flooded with light, so that you can know and understand the hope to which He has called you, and how rich is His glorious inheritance in the saints (His set-apart ones).
> —EPHESIANS 1:17–18, AMP, EMPHASIS ADDED

Look at this wonderful prayer Paul prayed for us by the unction of the Holy Ghost. He was asking God to grant wisdom and revelation from His holy Word. Why, Paul?

That the eyes of our *understanding* would be enlightened.

The word *understanding* is translated from the Greek word *dianoia*, which means "deep thought, imagination, or mind." The amplified version of the Bible translates *understanding* as *heart*, which makes sense because imagination is the deep thought of the heart. So wisdom and revelation of God's Word floods our imagination and forms those *thoughts* or *light* into ideas and plans according to the will of God.

David tells us in Psalm 119:130:

> The entrance of thy words giveth light; it giveth understanding unto the simple (KJV).

Why is it so important to God that our imagination be filled with his light?

Here's why, that we may know the hope of His calling. "Hope" means *expectation* of His calling. The Message Bible says it this way:

> So that you can see exactly what it is he is calling you to do.
> —EPHESIANS 1:15, THE MESSAGE

If we all had our imaginations filled with God's light from His Word, there wouldn't be so many confused and unsure believers. So many believers are floating from church to church trying to get a word so they will know what God is calling them to do. I preached a message a few years back called Misplaced Joints. Misplaced joints prevent the body from moving correctly and cause believers to be out of position and therefore out of God's purpose. Just get God's Word deep in your heart and keep it there and then you will see

God's plan, and then you will know God's plan, by vision, perception, and inner witness. God has a divine plan for each of us, and He deeply desires to reveal it to us through His Living Word. Peter tells us that God has already given us everything that pertains unto life and godliness through the knowledge of God. Everything we need to live the abundant overflowing life Jesus died to give is in His Holy Word. God's Word is eternal so it can speak to your past, present, and future. The Word will speak to you and show you things to come. It will show you the hope of His calling. God wants us to know what He requires of us; we have to allow His Word to richly dwell in us.

> And he brought him forth abroad, and said, Look
> now toward heaven, and tell the stars, if thou be
> able to number them: and he said unto him, So
> shall thy seed be.
> —GENESIS 15:5, KJV

Here we have God encouraging Abraham to use his imagination. Look at the stars, so shall your seed be. God gave Abraham a visual picture of the church of the firstborn, which was built centuries later. I believe Abraham looked up at all those stars every night and said, "Look at all my sons and daughters." That physical picture of the stars, along with the supernatural word (so shall thy seed be) planted in Abraham's imagination, was enough to sustain him for many years while he waited for the promise in faith. Years later God assisted His faith by changing his name from Abram to Abraham, meaning "father of many nations." Imagine all in his community calling this fatherless man "father of many nations." They were calling those things that are not as though they are. There is power in the words of God's children when they say what He's already proclaimed.

15

> These all died in faith, not having received the
> promises, but having seen them afar off, and were
> persuaded of them, and embraced them.
>
> —HEBREWS 11:13, KJV

Abraham died in faith—not doubt, not unbelief. He died yet believing that his seed would cover the Earth. He did not receive it or see it with his physical eyes, but he saw it *afar off* in his imagination. He imagined God. To imagine God is to imagine His eternal Word. God's Word will show you the riches of the glory of His inheritance in the saints. God will show you things to come when you allow His Word to fill your mind day and night. He sent His Word to be planted in our minds to accomplish the things He sent it to accomplish, and remember that God said it would not return to Him void.

Chapter 4
SPEAK NO EVIL

This book of the law shall not depart out of thy mouth;
but thou shalt meditate therein day and night, that
thou mayest observe to do according to all that is
written therein: for then thou shalt make thy way
prosperous, and then thou shalt have good success.

JOSHUA 1:8, KJV

GOD PROMISES US prosperity and good success if we follow these principles. Notice God doesn't promise success, He promises good success. Good success is ordained by our heavenly Father and it will last. The world can offer success, but it's not "good success" because it is not always connected with kingdom purposes.

> The blessing of the LORD, it maketh rich, and he addeth no sorrow with it.
> —PROVERBS 10:22, KJV

There are so many successful people who are depressed, unhappy, miserable, and angry. Our Bible tells us there is no peace for the wicked. Their success does not include God; they don't even know Him, but our loving heavenly Father wants us to have good, long-lasting success.

> Let the Lord be magnified, which hath pleasure in
> the prosperity of His servant.
>
> —Psalm 35:27, kjv

> Beloved, I wish above all things that thou
> mayest prosper and be in health, even as thy soul
> prospereth.
>
> —3 John 1:2, kjv

> But thou shalt remember the Lord thy God: for it
> is he that giveth thee power to get wealth.
>
> —Deuteronomy 8:18, kjv

God gives us the ability to get wealth, and this ability comes from His wisdom. God's wisdom is found in His Word, but we must find out how to extract it.

Joshua 1:8 is a spiritual law that God designed to cause us to prosper in all we do. First He tells us:

> This book of the law shall not depart out of thy
> mouth (kjv).

> Death and life are in the power of the tongue.
>
> —Proverbs 18:21, kjv

This scripture tells us our words have power, and we have power to speak death or life, blessings or curses. Jesus tells us in John 6:63:

> The words I speak unto you, they are spirit and
> they are life (kjv).

When we speak God's Word in faith we are bringing God's Spirit and God's life into the physical world. We are only able to speak God's Word in faith when it becomes part of us and one way to know that it's part of us is that we've memorized it. Once God's Word is memorized, it's there for the Holy Spirit to pull up whenever He desires. Remember, Jesus said that the "Holy Spirit, whom the Father will send in My name, He will teach you all things, and bring to your remembrance all things that I said to you" (John 14:26, NKJV). So that tells us that the Holy Spirit speaks to us from things we've heard from God's Word. When someone tells me they never hear from God, the first thing I ask them is, are you in the Word— are you hearing, reading, studying, and paying attention in church? God's Holy Spirit and God's eternal life are contained within His Holy Word. When we proclaim God's Word in the darkness of this world, darkness must give way to light.

In John 16:13, Jesus says:

> Howbeit when he, the Spirit of truth, is come, he
> will guide you into all truth (KJV).

Now in John 17:17, Jesus prays:

> Sanctify them through thy truth: thy word is truth
> (KJV).

So the Spirit of Truth is the Spirit of the Word. That means that *truth* and *the Word* are interchangeable.

> *You shall know the Word and the Word shall make*
> *you free* (see John 8:32, KJV).

Listen to John testify about Jesus Christ, the Word made flesh.

> That which was from the beginning, which we
> have heard, which we have seen with our eyes,
> which we have looked upon, and our hands have
> handled, concerning the Word of life—the life was
> manifested, and we have seen, and bear witness,

and declare to you that eternal life which was with
the Father and was manifested to us.

—1 JOHN 1:1–2, NKJV

In Him was life, and the life was the light of men.

—JOHN 1:4, NKJV

The *life* translates from the Greek word *Zoe*, which means "life
as God has it."

I don't believe God is sick.
I don't believe God is poor.
I don't believe God is afraid.
I don't believe God is confused.
I don't believe God is depressed.
I don't believe God is worried.

Neither should we be any of those things because we have God's
Word and His Spirit, and His eternal life is released when we proclaim His Word. God is telling Joshua, *"Keep my Word in your
mouth because son, when you speak my Word in the Earth, I manifest,
and when I manifest so does heaven's host"* (author's paraphrase). Isn't
that amazing? All you have to do is speak the scriptures, and our
great God and His holy angels are present. Heaven shows up when
the church of Jesus Christ proclaims God's Holy Word. Listen you
don't have to live depressed, fearful, stressed out, or confused, just
start proclaiming what God says about you in the Bible and God
will show up to perform His Word because He magnified His Word
above His holy name and he watches over His Word and hastens to
perform it. That's why I pray after every message I preach that God
would confirm His Word with signs, wonders, and miracles. What
we must realize is that after the Word of God is preached under the

anointing of the Holy Ghost anything is possible. We've got to get to the point we believe it.

> Therefore shall ye lay up these my words in your heart and in your soul, and bind them for a sign upon your hand, that they may be as frontlets between your eyes. And ye shall teach them your children, speaking of them when thou sittest in thine house, and when thou walkest by the way, when thou liest down, and when thou risest up. And thou shalt write them upon the door posts of thine house, and upon thy gates: That your days may be multiplied, and the days of your children, in the land which the LORD sware unto your fathers to give them, *as the days of heaven upon the earth.*
> —DEUTERONOMY 11:18–21, KJV, EMPHASIS ADDED

Glory! Heaven invades Earth when we the people of God proclaim His Holy Word in the Earth.

I remember years back when I was newly saved and full of that new zeal. My brother and I were out fishing on beautiful Lake Ladue in northeast Ohio. It just so happened they rented small boats, so I brought along my small, but efficient trolling motor. When we set out at daybreak, the water was smooth as glass, but as the morning progressed the waves started kicking up and the next thing we knew, the small boat was being tossed around. It quickly got to the point that our lives were in danger because of the wind and the waves pushing us into the dam. Then suddenly the Holy Spirit rose up in me, and at the top of my voice I yelled, "PEACE BE STILL IN THE NAME OF JESUS CHRIST!" This all took place so fast, I did not have time to even analyze speaking to the wind, I just did it. Sometimes we give the circumstances we go through power they don't deserve. God is in control and that's all there is to it! The Holy Spirit did not give me time to do like Peter and focus on the mighty waves and take my eyes off Jesus. I was lifted up off my feet in a small rocking boat and declared to the wind it must stop in Jesus' name. And within four or five seconds the wind came to a slow halt and we were able to return to shore safely. Remember, I was just a babe in Christ, so the whole event seemed like a dream but it really happened. Praise God it was not my time to die! Death and life are in the power of the tongue and when you have the Spirit of the Living God abiding within you, all things are possible.

We need to be careful of the words that come out of our mouths; just as heaven responds to the words of our mouths, so does hell with its demons. For so long we've cursed ourselves with our words, saying things like "you know cancer runs in my family" and "Uncle John just died from it, I guess I'm next." Remember, "death and life are in the power of the tongue" (Prov. 18:21, KJV). Here's another popular one, "you know nothing good ever happens to me." You need to call those words back by saying, "In the name of Jesus Christ, I cancel those words and render them fruitless!" Speaking God's Word brings goodness and mercy into your life, but speaking evil words over your life will give the devil a way in. God gave us authority in the Earth and authority is released by commands—commands are words. How does a king or a judge exercise their authority? It's through words. Seeing that we are made in the image of God, there is a certain level of creative power in our words. So let us speak blessings not curses.

> Death and life are in the power of the tongue: and
> they that love it shall eat the fruit thereof.
> —PROVERBS 18:21, KJV

> But I say unto you, That every idle word that men
> shall speak, they shall give account thereof in the
> day of judgment.
> —MATTHEW 12:36, KJV

Out of the same mouth proceedeth blessing and cursing. My brethren, these things ought not to be so.

—JAMES 3:10, KJV

Chapter 5

THINK NO EVIL

*This book of the law shall not depart out of thy mouth;
but thou shalt meditate therein day and night, that
thou mayest observe to do according to all that is
written therein: for then thou shalt make thy way
prosperous, and then thou shalt have good success.*

JOSHUA 1:8, KJV, EMPHASIS ADDED

Now GOD SWITCHES from Joshua's mouth to his mind.
God tells Joshua to meditate on His Word day and night.
The English word *meditate* comes from the Hebrew word
hagah, which means "to ponder and imagine." When we ponder on
a thought, we think on it over and over until it gets deep within
us. This is what God is instructing Joshua to do— meditate on His
Word day and night. Once we get passages of scripture deep within
us, we begin to imagine it; we begin to see it coming to pass in
our imaginations. Once we know certain scriptures from meditating
on them, faith is built within us because we're beginning to trust.
We seem to trust what and who we know. We cannot really trust
God without having knowledge of Him, and we obtain knowledge
of God through His Word. The more we become familiar with God
the more we trust God. Now as faith grows, we begin to see the
Word within our imagination because words describe images, and
inner images are seen within our imagination. But these aren't nor-
mal images, they're supernatural images because their origin is God
(His Word). It's our human nature to trust people and things we

know and feel good about. We get to know God through His Word, and the greater knowledge we have of His Word, the greater knowledge we have of Him. The more we know Him, the easier it is to trust Him, and as we develop greater trust we gain greater vision. Words paint pictures in our imaginations, pictures of things we have knowledge of. Try this—close your eyes—imagine a red convertible Corvette Stingray with white interior. See it. The only way you were able to see that car is you knew the colors red and white. Plus, you knew what a convertible Corvette Stingray looks like and you knew what it was. The more we ponder or meditate on God's Word, the more we know it and trust it. Soon we will be able to see the manifestation of it in our imagination. Then once we see it inside, faith is there to bring it forth into the physical realm because we trust God, plus we've already witnessed it inside our imaginations.

Faith is the evidence of something unseen. Hebrews 11:1 says it's unseen in the physical realm, but it's seen in our imagination. Remember, our imagination is the place of forming and conception. God's Word, like seed, is planted in the soil of our mind, and the more it's watered over and over, it will soon spring up and be visible in our imaginations.

> This book of the law shall not depart out of thy mouth; but thou shalt meditate therein day and night, that thou mayest observe to do according to all that is written therein: for then thou shalt make thy way prosperous, and then thou shalt have good success.
>
> —JOSHUA 1:8, KJV

> Blessed is the man Who walks not in the counsel of the ungodly, Nor stands in the path of sinners, Nor sits in the seat of the scornful; But his delight is in the law of the Lord, And in His law he meditates day and night. He shall be like a tree Planted

by the rivers of water, That brings forth its fruit in
its season, Whose leaf also shall not wither; And
whatever he does shall prosper.

—PSALM 1:1–3, NKJV

Both of these tremendous promises have the same instruction:
meditate on God's Word day and night.

Meditate means in the Hebrew "to ponder," "to imagine." Let's
review the wonderful benefits of meditation.

The eyes of your understanding being enlightened;
that you may know what is the hope of His calling,
what are the riches of the glory of His inheritance
in the saints.

—EPHESIANS 1:18, NKJV, EMPHASIS ADDED

These all died in faith, not having received the
promises, *but having seen them afar off,* and were
persuaded of them, and embraced them, and
confessed that they were strangers and pilgrims on
the earth.

—HEBREWS 11:13, KJV, EMPHASIS ADDED

This book of the law shall not depart out of thy
mouth; but thou shalt meditate therein day and
night, that thou mayest observe to do according to
all that is written therein: for *then thou shalt make
thy way prosperous, and then thou shalt have good
success.*

—JOSHUA 1:8, KJV, EMPHASIS ADDED

He shall be like a tree Planted by the rivers of water,
That brings forth its fruit in its season, Whose leaf

also shall not wither; And *whatever he does shall prosper.*

—PSALM 1:1–3, NKJV, EMPHASIS ADDED

I beseech you therefore, brethren, by the mercies of God, that you present your bodies a living sacrifice, holy, acceptable to God, which is your reasonable service. And do not be conformed to this world, but be transformed by the renewing of your mind, *that you may prove what is that good and acceptable and perfect will of God.*

—ROMANS 12:2, NKJV, EMPHASIS ADDED

Just begin to think on God's promises day and night. You'll begin to see them manifest first in your imagination, then in your physical life. God's Word is designed to prosper us and bring us good success.

Biblical meditation is intimate fellowship with our Creator. John 1:1 tells us, "The Word was God," and the English word *word* comes from the Greek word *logos*, which means "the thought."

God is the Word.
God is the logos.
God is "the thought."
God is "His thought."

You are your thoughts; what's closer to you? What's always been with you? You are your thoughts. As a man thinketh in his heart so is he. When we meditate on scripture, we're allowing God's thoughts to mingle with our thoughts, and that's intimate fellowship. Nothing is closer to you than your thoughts; now nothing is closer to you than God. You want to be close to God? Start to ponder on His Word over and over, day and night and God will draw near to you as you draw near to Him.

For it is God who works in you both to will and to
do for His good pleasure.
—PHILIPPIANS 2:13, NKJV

I will meditate on Your precepts, And contemplate
Your ways.
—PSALM 119:15, NKJV

Oh, how I love Your law! It is my meditation all
the day.
—PSALM 119:97, NKJV

I have more understanding than all my teachers,
For Your testimonies are my meditation.
—PSALM 119:99, NKJV

May my meditation be sweet to Him; I will be glad
in the Lord.
—PSALM 104:34, NKJV

My eyes are awake through the night watches, That
I may meditate on Your word.
—PSALM 119:148, NKJV

David understood the importance of meditating on God's Word.
David understood the fellowship and sweet communion of meditating on God's Word. This I believe was one of the keys to David's
success as a man of God. To be after God's heart is to be after His
thoughts, after His Word.

If you're going through a season of lack or if you need money for
bills or your ministry, let's meditate day and night on God's Word
and watch the promised prosperity manifest.

I have given and it shall be given to me, pressed down, shaken together, and running over shall men give unto me (see Luke 6:38).

God will make all grace abound toward me (see 2 Corinthians 9:8).

My God shall supply all my need according to His riches in glory by Christ Jesus (see Philippians 4:19).

God gives me power to get wealth (see Deuteronomy 8:18).

The Lord is my Shepherd, I shall not want (see Psalm 23:1).

Meditate on these scriptures. Think on them over and over day and night and as you become familiar with them and memorize them, you will begin to trust the Word. By doing that, the Word will get deep within you and then you will start to see yourself out of debt, blessed financially in your imagination, and when you see it on the inside, faith comes. With faith comes wisdom and wisdom will provide your plan to bring forth the manifestation of what you hoped for and more!

Let's say you've got health problems or a bad report from the doctor.

Jesus Christ is the Lord that healeth me (see Exodus 15:26).

Jesus Christ heals all my diseases (see Psalm 103:3).

I will prosper and be in good health, even as my soul prospers (see 3 John: 2).

Jesus Christ bore my sins in His own body on the tree and by His stripes I was healed. (see 1 Peter 2:24).

First Peter 2:24 tells us we were healed at the cross two thousand years ago. The way to believe something that hasn't happened in the natural is to see it in the spiritual, and that happens when we meditate on these passages. The longer you meditate on these healing scriptures, the better chance of seeing them manifest in your imagination and then your physical body. Let's say someone you care about is sick and they need prayer.

In Jesus' name I lay hands on the sick and they recover (see Mark 16:18).

I've prayed the prayer of faith and the Lord will raise them up (see James 5:15).

The effective, fervent prayer of the righteous one avails much (see James 5:16).

Let's say the devil is attacking your mind

In Jesus' name I cast out devils (see Mark 16:17).

For God has not given me the spirit of fear, but of power, love, and of a sound mind (see 2 Timothy 1:7).

I have authority to tread on serpents and scorpions and over all the power of the devil (see Luke 10:19).

No weapon formed against me shall prosper, and every tongue that rises against me in judgment I condemn (see Isaiah 54:17).

Confess and meditate on these verses until they become a part of you and the devil will flee! Do just what Jesus did when he was sent by the Holy Spirit into the wilderness. It is written!

Let's say you're beginning to doubt yourself and your ability to perform a task.

> *I can do all things through Christ who strengthens me (see Philippians 4:13).*

> *Thanks be to God who always causes me to triumph in Christ (see 2 Corinthians 2:14).*

> *All things are possible to me for I believe God (see Mark 9:23).*

Just meditate day and night on these scriptures and soon you'll see yourself excelling and prospering in all you do.

> *And whatever he does shall prosper (see Psalm 1:3).*

> Let's say something bad has happened and you're beginning to stress out.

> *God will keep me in perfect peace as my mind stays on Him because I trust in Him (see Isaiah 26:3).*

> *I will trust in the Lord with all my heart and I won't lean to my own understanding. In all my ways I will acknowledge Him and He will direct my path (see Proverbs 3:5–6).*

> *I will pray and the peace of God which passeth all understanding shall guard my heart and mind through Jesus Christ (see Philippians 4:7).*

*And I know that all things work together for my good
because I love God and I am called according to His purpose
(see Romans 8:28).*

Ponder on God's Word and soon you will begin to imagine the thing hoped for, and then you will have evidence of the unseen. And then by faith you will receive your healing, your deliverance, your breakthrough, your blessing in Jesus' name. Amen.

Meditation on God's Word causes it to sink deep into our imagination—the place where thoughts form into ideas, plans, and dreams. Look at Hebrews 8:10:

> For this is the covenant that I will make with the house of Israel after those days, says the Lord: I will put My laws in their mind and write them on their hearts; and I will be their God, and they shall be My people (NKJV).

Notice God says, "I will put My laws in their mind." The English word *mind* is translated from the Green word *dianoia*, which means "deep thought" and it's also translated from the word *imagination*. Remember, the imagination is where plans and ideas are formed. This is also the place where dreams and visions are birthed good and evil. It was an evil imagination that provoked God into destroying the first world. God's desire in the Old and the New Covenant is to put His Word deep into our imaginations. Look, we find this word *dianoia* again in Matthew 22:37:

> Jesus said unto him, Thou shalt love the Lord thy God with all thy heart, and with all thy soul, and with all thy mind. This is the first and great commandment (KJV).

We are to love God with all our "deep thoughts," with all our imaginations. The only way this can happen is through His Word. The only way we can love God is through His Word because the only way we can know God is through His Word. You can't really love someone you don't know. So many people confess they love the Lord, but they don't know His Word. Jesus tells us the way to love Him is through obedience to His Word.

> We love Him because He first loved us.
> —1 JOHN 4:19, NKJV

The only way we know the love of God is through the Bible. If we love His Word, we love Him. If we don't have time for His Word, we don't have time for Him. If we despise his Word, we despise Him. The more we fill ourselves with God's Word, the more we fill ourselves with God.

> Let the Word of Christ dwell in you richly in all wisdom, teaching and admonishing one another in psalms and hymns and spiritual songs, singing with grace in your hearts to the Lord.
> —COLOSSIANS 3:16, NKJV

Chapter 6

THE BATTLEGROUND

THERE'S AN OLD saying, "The idle mind is the devil's playground." Notice the mind is called "ground." Even the Bible calls our mind "ground."

In Matthew 13:23, Jesus says:

> But he who received seed on the good ground is he who hears the word and understands *it,* who indeed bears fruit and produces: some a hundred-fold, some sixty, some thirty (NKJV).

In this parable the seed is God's Word and the good ground is a good mind. But notice Jesus describes a good mind as one who hears God's Word and then understands it. The English word *understand* is translated from the Greek Word *suniemi,* which means to "put together" or "form." Think about it—we form conclusions after we've thought something through. This is biblical meditation. The more we go over scripture in our mind, the greater understanding we receive. Sometimes I ask my church members if they remember what the sermon was two hours after service and some don't remember. What happens is, once service is over, we fail to meditate on what we've received and we lose it, causing us to be unfruitful for the kingdom. So Jesus is telling us that a good mind or good ground hears the Word of God and meditates on it. Then that mind will indeed be fruitful. This is found in Joshua 1:8, which we studied earlier (*meditate day and night and you will find good success and prosperity*). Remember, biblical meditation brings inner visualization—then physical manifestation.

In the Parable of the Sower, Jesus likens our mind to soil or ground. We are to sow God's Word into this soil or ground. Once it's sown, we must meditate on it; then it will bring forth fruit that glorifies God. Now just as God commanded Adam to guard or protect the Garden of Eden (Gen. 2:15), Proverbs 4:23 tells us to:

> Keep and guard your heart with all vigilance and
> above all that you guard, for out of it flows springs
> of life (AMP).

This scripture doesn't say, "Above all, guard your house or your money, or even your family." It says to guard your heart with all vigilance and above all else. Why? Because this is where the devil attacks us, and our imagination is where ideas, plans, hopes, dreams, and conclusions are formed.

The English dictionary defines *imagine* as "the forming of mental pictures." This is the place where either demonic lies or God's truth directs our lives. Let's look again at the Parable of the Sower in Matthew 13:18–19:

> Therefore hear the parable of the sower: When
> anyone hears the word of the kingdom, and does
> not understand *it*, then the wicked *one* comes and
> snatches away what was sown in his heart. This is
> he who received seed by the wayside (NKJV).

We've already established that because of the evil imagination we're all born with, the devil has access to our imagination. This will be so until we're gone from this physical body. But God's Word will limit and expose the devil's lies as long as we allow it to abide in our hearts. God's Word abides in our imaginations when we meditate on it. You see, the more we go over it in our minds, the deeper it sinks in and eventually takes root. The devil can only steal what we haven't pondered on, what we don't meditate on. God's Word takes root in our imagination when we meditate on it. Matthew 13:21 says:

Yet it has no real root in him, but is temporary
(inconstant, lasts but a little while); and when affliction or trouble or persecution comes on account
of the Word, at once he is caused to stumble [he
is repelled and begins to distrust and desert Him
Whom he ought to trust and obey] and he falls
away (AMP).

This is the story happening in churches everywhere all the time.
People are hearing the Word everywhere—in churches, on televi-
sion, in books, on CDs, on DVD, and on the radio. Then affliction
and trouble from the devil (because of the Word) come, and because God's people have not allowed the Word to take root in them
through biblical meditation, they fall away from trusting God and
are defeated.

For though we walk in the flesh, we do not war
according to the flesh. For the weapons of our
warfare are not carnal but mighty in God for
pulling down strongholds, casting down arguments
and every high thing that exalts itself against the
knowledge of God, bringing every thought into
captivity to the obedience of Christ, and being
ready to punish all disobedience when your obedience is fulfilled.
—2 CORINTHIANS 10:3–6, NKJV

Let me say that the main weapon we have against demonic attacks in our minds is the sword of the Spirit, which is the Word
of God. This is how Jesus defeated the devil in the wilderness, and
this is how we are to combat those lies from the wicked one. Simply
"It is written." The Word is our greatest weapon against demonic
lies. When Jesus dealt with the devil in the wilderness, He spoke
God's Word and ran the devil off. It's very difficult to run a bad

thought out of your mind with another thought. It's much easier with audible words. Remember, Jesus told us to "talk to the mountain" and Jesus "cursed the fig tree out loud." When evil thoughts and images enter your mind, cast them out in Jesus' name! Speak out loud with authority! Paul tells us the weapons of our warfare are mighty through God. God's Word is only a weapon in the hand of the Holy Ghost (Sword of the Spirit). The unsaved man can quote scripture, but it will lack power. But the spirit-filled child of God can speak and proclaim God's Word in the power of the Holy Ghost. All of the other parts of armor are defensive—shield of faith, helmet of salvation, breastplate of righteousness, shoes of peace, and then comes our offensive weapon, the Sword of the Spirit—the Word of God. Start casting down those vain imaginations with God's Word. A vain imagination is the forming of evil thoughts. And once evil thoughts are formed, a stronghold is erected in your mind. When the devil has a stronghold in the mind, the victims are willed to do evil because they're convinced they have to do wrong. Strongholds usually take time to build. You see, the devils don't have anything else to do except harass humans. If you keep telling the same lie over and over, sooner or later you're going to believe the lie. If you keep sinning over and over, soon you will lose control of yourself.

Romans 6:16 tells us:

> Know ye not, that to whom ye yield yourselves servants to obey, his servants ye are to whom ye obey; whether of sin unto death, or of obedience unto righteousness? (KJV).

Strongholds can be torn down by God's Word and prayer, but the danger in this is that some people have had them so long, they hold on to them. They're afraid to be delivered. The devil deceives them with his lies:

- It's too late. God's not going to forgive you. You will never be able to stop doing this.

- Do you realize how lonely you will be without them?

Once those lies have been meditated on long enough, you will start to visualize them in your imagination.

Webster's dictionary defines *imagine* as "to form mental pictures." Words create pictures and images, and demonic words create pictures of destruction and ruin in our imaginations. So we must be quick to cast down wicked thoughts and imaginations. Please don't meditate on evil; meditate on God's Word:

> Finally, brethren, whatsoever things are true, whatsoever things are honest, whatsoever things are just, whatsoever things are pure, whatsoever things are lovely, whatsoever things are of good report; if there be any virtue, and if there be any praise, think on these things.
> —PHILIPPIANS 4:8, KJV

Let's continue to look at the parable of the sower:

> But he that received the seed into stony places, the same is he that heareth the word, and anon with joy receiveth it; Yet hath he not root in himself, but dureth for a while: for when tribulation or persecution ariseth because of the word, by and by he is offended.
> —MATTHEW 13:20–21, KJV

I can't count how many times saints of God leave our services on fire, full of excitement and joy only to lose it the next day. This passage tells why; the reason is they have no root in themselves. God's Word planted in the soil of our minds must remain there long enough to take root. It needs water and light, and it comes by way of meditation. We must ponder on the scriptures over and over in the mind until roots or revelations expand deep in our minds. You see it's not enough to listen to the Word on Sunday morning and then go on about our business; we need to write those verses down and take them home and meditate on them until they stick. Without doing that we won't be able to endure the attacks from the devil, which include tribulation and persecution.

Tribulation is translated from the Greek word *thlip-sis,* which means "pressure," "burden," and "trouble." Pressure on your job, pressure making ends meet, bearing burdens of your own as well as for family and friends, trouble after trouble. Does any of that sound familiar? Not all bad things that happen to us are from the devil, but Jesus gives us a hint as to when they are, "they arise!" They come from nowhere, they're unexpected, and they usually come when you're doing good! Good times can be dangerous times because our guards are down and our prayer life is lacking. But most importantly these demonic attacks come because of the Word you just received on Sunday. This shows me how important the Word is to us. This scripture doesn't say the devil attacks us because we went to church or sang hymns or praised God, worshiped God, or got in the prayer line. He attacks us for fear that we might get that Word and meditate on it and begin to build more trust in God, and then allow the Word to go deep into our imagination where we then begin to see ourselves as God sees us, victorious, full of power and love. Once that happens the devil is afraid our imagination might reveal to us images of us doing great exploits for the kingdom in line with the will of God as we step out and do them. My friend, that's what the devil fears more than anything else, the church doing the will of the Father. Jesus told His disciples when they were hungry, *"My food is to do the will of Him who sent Me"* (John 4:34). Doing God's will was Jesus' entire existence. Should it not be the same with us? What

I find so wonderful about this parable is that it all starts with seed, the Word of God. Let's continue with this great parable.

> He also that received seed among the thorns is he
> that heareth the word; and the care of this world,
> and the deceitfulness of riches, choke the word,
> and he becometh unfruitful.
>
> —MATTHEW 13:22, KJV

Let's look at this verse closely. These people received God's Word but they received with a mind full of worries and a mind full of lust for things. Let me take a moment to stress the importance of receiving the Word properly.

> Enter into his gates with thanksgiving, and into
> his courts with praise: be thankful unto him, and
> bless his name.
>
> —PSALM 100:4, KJV

First we must develop an appreciation for God's Word. Ancient Israel rejoiced at the fact that they possessed the living Word. You see, they realized it set them apart from the other nations because within the Word is supreme wisdom and understanding. We should have thankful hearts when we enter the sanctuary or private Bible study time. Then we should offer up praise to God because praise will clear our minds from all the worry, stress, and anxiety associated with this fallen world we presently live in. As we magnify God, we begin to realize the stuff that's consuming us is so small compared to the mighty God we serve. James tells us to receive God's Word with meekness—that means with a humble heart. In this parable Jesus tells us that worry and lust will chock the Word out of our mind just like weeds take over your garden if you don't remove them.

Let's look at good ground or a good mind prepared to receive God's Word. "But that on the good ground are they, which in an honest and good heart, having heard the word, keep it, and bring forth fruit with patience" (Luke 8:15, KJV). Notice a good mind that bears fruit for God's kingdom hears the Word and keeps it. The Greek word *katecho,* which is translated to the English word *keep* means "to hold on to by memorizing." Because saints of old took God's Word and meditated on it, they bore fruit with patience. Bearing fruit means living a productive life within the parameters of the will of God. And this productivity is in the natural realm and the spiritual realm—the mind. But notice Jesus tells us that they bear fruit with patience. This indicates to us meditation on the Word will release patience in our lives, and how we need that. Patience is the ability to endure; remember the old saying "God's Word will keep you." That saying was birthed from testimonies of how keeping your mind filled with the living Word would enable you to make it through the storms of life. Nobody really understood how the Word was able to do that; most didn't care. But let me tell you it's worked for me in my life, and I believe that endurance is released when God's Word enters the imagination through meditation. It's there we see ourselves coming out. Now you don't always have to have a mental picture of your victory; God's Word can give you discernment or a strong impression that you're going to make it. Patience is also endurance with a good attitude, going through without murmuring, complaining, anger, and bitterness. Not everyone can do that, but those who have been kept by the power of God's Word endure in love. The mind is the battleground.

Chapter 7

SWEET COMMUNION

Wherefore lay apart all filthiness and superfluity of naughtiness, and receive with meekness the engrafted word, which is able to save your souls.

JAMES 1:21, KJV

ENGRAFTING GOD'S WORD deep into your heart is engrafting God himself deep in your thoughts, and your imagination abides within the depths of the thoughts of your heart. God is His Word.

> In the beginning was the Word, and the Word was with God, the Word was God.
>
> —JOHN 1:1, KJV

God cannot be separated from His Word. When we engraft God's Word in our minds, we engraft God into our minds. Look what we're promised when we do that:

> Thou wilt keep him in perfect peace, whose mind is stayed on thee: because he trusteth in thee.
>
> —ISAIAH 26:3, KJV

To keep your mind stayed on God is to keep your mind stayed on His Word. The way we keep our mind on God is by meditating on His Word. Outside of God's Word we have no knowledge of

God. Having your mind filled with God's Word will cause you to better understand Him and His ways.

> For my thoughts are not your thoughts, neither are your ways my ways, saith the LORD. For as the heavens are higher than the earth, so are my ways higher than your ways, and my thoughts than your thoughts.
> —ISAIAH 55:8–9, KJV

God thinks and acts differently than we do, yet He gives us an opportunity to learn how He thinks and acts through His Word. As we begin to think as He does, we will begin to act as He does.

> For as he thinketh in his heart, so is he.
> —PROVERBS 23:7, KJV

We must learn to meditate and confess God's Word daily because this and only this will release the abundant life Jesus came to give us.

> I am come that they might have life, and that they might have it more abundantly.
> —JOHN 10:10, KJV

The God kind of life, *Zoe,* comes from God's Word. The only way for us to live as God lives is to think like God thinks, then we will do as God does. Look what Jesus tells us to do in Matthew 5:48:

> Be ye therefore perfect, even as your Father which is in heaven is perfect (KJV).

The English word *perfect* comes from the Greek work *teleios,* which means "completeness." This word expresses maturity. When we begin to think as God thinks and act as God acts, we then begin the process of perfection. Why? It is because God is perfect in all His ways. You see, it's an honor to possess God's Words in our hearts because the Word will transform into His image. Then we will begin to mature because of the Word. Let's look at John 6:63:

> It is the Spirit who gives life; the flesh profits nothing. The words that I speak to you are spirit, and *they* are life (NKJV).

The Holy Spirit gives life to God's Word; therefore, God's Word is a living Word. Seeing that God's Word is alive, God's Word speaks; God's Word breathes; God's Word sees; God's Word hears. It's a living Word! This will revolutionize your thinking. The Bible is not just a book, the Bible is a person, and the person is the Lord Jesus Christ. Now I'm not talking about the materials your Bible is made of being a person, I'm talking about the Spirit of the Word that's written.

> For the word of God is living and powerful, and sharper than any two-edged sword, piercing even to the division of soul and spirit, and of joints and marrow, and is a discerner of the thoughts and intents of the heart.
> —Hebrews 4:12, NKJV

The Holy Spirit within God's Word speaks to us in our minds. God's Word is the vehicle by which the Holy Spirit enters the believer, so that means being filled with the Spirit is also being filled with the Word. Look at 1 Peter 1:23:

> Being born again, not of corruptible seed, but of incorruptible, by the word of God, which liveth and abideth forever (KJV).

Even at conversion, it's God's Word that makes us born again. And God's life within His Word does the work within us. God's living Word speaks to us when we meditate on it. As we ponder on God's Word we hear that still small voice; we see visions and dreams because the Holy Spirit is the Spirit of the Word. Listen to Jesus, the Word of God, speak to us in Revelation 3:20:

> Behold, I stand at the door, and knock: if any man hear my voice, and open the door, I will come in to him, and will sup with him, and he with me (KJV).

Notice Jesus says, "I will come into him." Jesus is saying if you open the door to your mind, He will come into your mind. I believe He's talking to His children when He says, I am standing at the door knocking. They can't hear Jesus' knocking because their minds are so full of vain imaginations, problems, worries, and stress. Ephesians 3:17 tells us that Christ dwells in our hearts by faith. Our heart is our mind, where thoughts and imaginations exist. So Jesus, the Word, says to us that if we will hear His gentle knocking, He will enter our thoughts and sup with us. The supper table is a place where families fellowship, share, and enjoy each other's company. This sweet communion is where the living Word speaks revelation, releases wisdom, and gives us visual illustrations of our hopes and dreams according to the will of God. Let's look at Paul's prayer for us in 2 Corinthians 13:14:

> The grace of the Lord Jesus Christ, and the love of God, and the communion of the Holy Ghost, be with you all (KJV).

Paul is praying that the Church of Jesus would have communion with the Godhead, Father, Son, and the Holy Ghost. Now let's look

at what the Apostle John tells us about the unity of the Godhead in
1 John 5:7:

> For there are three that bear record in heaven, the
> Father, the Word, and the Holy Ghost: and these
> three are one (KJV).

Notice what John calls Jesus the one he loved, the one he walked
with daily for over three years, the one whom he laid his head upon
at the last supper.

THE WORD

So when we speak about fellowship within the Godhead, fellowship with God can be fellowship with the Word. Fellowship with
the Word is one of the main themes of this book. As you know we
cannot see the Holy Spirit or the Father with our natural eyes, but
we can gaze at God's Word all day and night if we choose, and that
is very intimate fellowship with our Creator in our hearts. Listen to
what John tell us in 1 John 1:7:

> But if we walk in the light, as he is in the light, we
> have fellowship one with another, and the blood
> of Jesus Christ His Son cleanseth us from all sin
> (KJV).

This scripture indicates to us that if we "walk" or "live our lives"
in the light, we have fellowship with the Lord because He's in the
light as well. The light talked about here is the Word of God. John is
talking about an inner fellowship that takes place deep in our heart
after meditating on the Word.

> The entrance of thy words giveth light; it giveth
> understanding unto the simple.
> —PSALM 119:130, KJV

47

> Thy Word is a lamp unto my feet, and a light and
> a light unto my path.
> —PSALM 119:105, KJV

Jesus is the Light and Jesus is the Word, and when we ponder on God's Word over and over, a sweet communion takes place between our natural thoughts and God's supernatural thoughts. And over a period of time we will begin to yield our old thought patterns to the thoughts of God. When this happens, our imagination will display new possibilities as well as new revelation for us according to the will of God. God's Word will cause us to see ourselves prospering, overcoming, and living in the realm of overflowing life. To walk in the light is to live in God's Word every single day of your life on Earth and to allow God's Word to live inside of you every single day of your life. God desires daily communion. He desires fellowship unbroken, not just on Sunday mornings, but every day by prayer, praise, worship, and meditation on His Holy Word.

Chapter 8

INNER WITNESS

*So then faith cometh by hearing, and hear-
ing by the Word of God.*

ROMANS 10:17, KJV

THIS PASSAGE TEACHES us that faith comes to us by hearing the Word of God. So that means when we fellowship
with Jesus, the living Word, He imparts faith to us. This all
takes place within our hearts, the place of thoughts and imagination.
Faith is believing God's Word before it manifests physically. Faith
is believing God's Word is truth, regardless of when it manifests in
this world. We believe it because God says it, period. But God in His
merciful kindness allows us to see things beforehand if we're in fellowship with His Word. This is what I call *inner witness*, and it takes
place in our imagination. Let's look at what the apostle Paul tells us
in 2 Corinthians 4:18:

> While we look not at the things which are seen,
> but at the things which are not seen: for the things
> which are seen are temporal; but the things which
> are not seen are eternal (KJV).

This is a spiritual principle. You see, the way we see things invisible to the physical eye is to see them within our imagination. Things
that are invisible naturally to us can be outside time, and the things
we see physically are held within time and subject to corruption.

God's Word will show us things that are *suspended* in the spiritual realm that we might know things to come. Now, when we see them, it takes faith and hope to bring about their physical manifestation in the physical realm.

Remember, the Spirit of Truth is also the Spirit of the Word.

> Howbeit when he, the Spirit of truth, is come, he
> will guide you into all truth: for he shall not speak
> of himself; but whatsoever he shall hear, that shall
> he speak: and he will shew you things to come.
> —JOHN 16:13, KJV

In this text there's a reason Jesus calls the Holy Spirit the "Spirit of Truth." I believe it's to draw our attention to God's Word, which in John 17:17 is called "truth." So Jesus is telling us that it's God's Spirit inside of His Word that tells us things to come. It's like the Word of God is a vehicle for the Holy Spirit to enter man's heart or thoughts. Remember, words are thoughts, thoughts are words. Filling our minds with God's Word and meditating on the Word we've received will enable the Holy Spirit to show us things to come. And when we see them within our imagination, there's faith to receive them. I remember during one of our home prayer meetings, the Holy Spirit showed me a man coming to my door carrying a huge Bible, so I kept praying and three minutes later this same man was at the door. He said he was looking for a home Bible study that was to be held on our street but this was not the right place. By then our house was filled with the glory of the Lord, so we invited him in. We began to pray over this man and he received a tremendous breakthrough. He began to prophesy and told us, by the Spirit of the Lord, never to stop this fervent prayer and that the Lord was well pleased with us. As he was leaving full of joy, he told us the only reason he stopped at our house was he saw the praise God license plates on all the cars in the driveway, but guess what, no one had praise God plates!

> Howbeit when he, the Spirit of truth, is come, he
> will guide you into all truth: for he shall not speak
> of himself; but whatsoever he shall hear, that shall
> he speak: and he will shew you things to come.
> —JOHN 16:13, KJV

> Now faith is the substance of things hoped for, the
> evidence of things not seen.
> —HEBREWS 11:1, KJV

The way we have evidence of something not seen physically is to see it in our imagination. Let's look at Jesus Christ, our example of how to walk by faith and not by sight.

> Most assuredly, I say to you, the Son can do
> nothing of Himself, but what He sees the Father
> do; for whatever He does, the Son also does in like
> manner.
> —JOHN 5:19, NKJV

Jesus is telling us He only releases faith in the things He sees the Father do first. Lazarus wasn't raised from the tomb twice, once by the Father, then by the Son. But evidently, Jesus saw it happen within His imagination, and when He saw it, He carried it out; for it was the Father's will according to the Father's Word. This is how God wants us to operate as well, but our minds must be filled continually with God's Word. The Word will show us, the Word will lead us, the Word will guide us. The Word is God, the Spirit of the Word is the Holy Spirit. The Word made flesh is Jesus Christ. There you have the Godhead, Father, Son, and Holy Spirit, one with the Word. Let's look at Proverbs 1:23: "Turn you at my reproof: behold, I will pour out my Spirit unto you, I will make known my words unto you" (KJV). This scripture is telling us to turn to the Word of God, and when we turn back to God's Word, God promises to pour out His

Spirit unto us. And this outpouring of God's Spirit will make God's Word known to us. This is the Spirit of Wisdom and Revelation. I believe this next outpouring of God's Spirit will be prompted by a turning back to God's Word. And when the church does that, God will pour out His Spirit upon us in a mighty, mighty way. And this outpouring of His Spirit will flood us with wisdom and knowledge and revelation from His Word. The Bible records several revivals that took place in ancient Israel because there was a turning to God's Word, and I believe this next one will be so.

> For I will pour water upon him that is thirsty, and floods upon the dry ground: I will pour my spirit upon thy seed. and my blessing upon thine offspring.
> —ISAIAH 44:3, KJV

This outpouring is for those who are thirsty for the living Word of God. Are you thirsty for the living Word of God? If you aren't, pray to God to please make you thirsty for His Word. He'll do it. I am sure He will. In this text He calls His Word "water," just like Paul does in Ephesians 5:26:

> That He might sanctify and cleanse her with the washing of water by the Word (NKJV).

God is ready to pour wisdom, revelation, and knowledge from His Word on anyone who's thirsty for His Word. Let's take a look at Joel 2:28–29:

> And it shall come to pass afterward, that I will pour out my Spirit upon all flesh (KJV).

Here we have God saying again, "I will pour out my Spirit," as we've seen in Proverbs 1:23 and Isaiah 44:3, when God pours out His Spirit, He's pouring out wisdom, knowledge, and revelation from His Holy Word.

> And your sons and your daughters shall prophesy (NKJV).

Prophesy is a result of God's Holy Word, and all prophesy should be in line with God's Word. The more God's Word abides in you, the greater chance you have of prophesying truth. Let's look at Romans 12:6:

> Having then gifts differing according to the grace that is given to us, whether prophecy, let us prophesy according to the proportion of faith (KJV).

Listen to what Paul is revealing to us—let us prophesy according to the size of our faith. The greater the faith, the greater the prophecy. In Romans 10:17 we find the following passage:

> So then faith cometh by hearing, and hearing by the Word of God (KJV).

So this means the greater your Word level, the greater your faith, and the greater your faith, the greater your prophecy. Let's go back to Joel 2:28–29 and finish looking at the effects of this great outpouring from our God. First it's prophecy. Then it's dreams and visions. Your old men shall dream dreams; your young men shall see visions.

Dreams and visions both occur within our imagination, the place where thoughts are formed into plans and ideas. This is the place of conception as we learned earlier. As we meditate on the Living Word, the Spirit of the Word will release dreams and visions according to the will of God. But understand this, everything we need, everything we receive from God starts with His Holy Word, which He has magnified above His Holy Name.

Chapter 9

THE LIVING WORD

Behold, I stand at the door and knock. If any-
one hears My voice and opens the door, I will come
in to him and dine with him, and he with Me.

REVELATION 3:20, NKJV

My son, keep thy father's commandment,
and forsake not the law of thy mother: Bind
them continually upon thine heart.

PROVERBS 6:20–21, KJV

GOD'S WISDOM IS telling us to bind God's Word to the thoughts in our mind. Now, to bind or tie, you must make a circular motion, and when a circle is completed, the end and the beginning are continuous. Circles represent repetition, in that you're covering the same area over and over. This is biblical meditation, and look at these three major benefits of meditating on God's Word in Proverbs 6:22:

When thou goest, it shall lead thee,

When thou sleepest, it shall keep thee,

When thou awakest, it shall talk with thee (KJV).

If you diligently fill your mind and meditate on God's living Word, the living Word will guide you, keep you, and talk to you. What more could we ask for from our heavenly Father? But it seems like we find time for everything else other than God's living Word, Jesus. We must keep in mind, God's Word is alive!

> For there are three that bear record in heaven, the Father, the Word, and the Holy Ghost: and these three are one.
>
> —1 JOHN 5:7, KJV

Now let's look at these tremendous truths concerning meditation on the Word of God.

Point A: "When thou goest, it shall lead thee."

One of the major problems the church is facing is confusion, and we know confusion is not of God. Being in the wrong place at the wrong time can be detrimental to us because God is a God of divine order. Most of the things Christians do today are things they never prayed about. Then once they get in the middle of situations, they ask for God to assist them in endeavors that He never ordained. Just because something looks promising doesn't necessarily mean it is. God is all-knowing and our success rate in life would be so much greater if we would take things before the Lord and tarry. God sometimes sends us to very unattractive situations to test our obedience and trust in Him. But rest assured, if God ordains something it shall prosper because it's the Lord's divine will. To be in the center of God's will for our lives, we must allow God to guide us to certain places at certain times. One sign to let us know we're in God's will is provision. God will always make provision for us when we're in His will. But we must be able to discern God's provision when He releases it to us. Sometimes it doesn't look like we think it should.

> And the word of the LORD came unto him, saying,
> Get thee hence, and turn thee eastward, and hide
> thyself by the brook Cherith, that is before Jordan.
> And it shall be, that thou shalt drink of the brook;
> and I have commanded the ravens to feed thee
> there.
> —1 KINGS 17:2–4, KJV

First of all, notice it was the Word that spoke to him.

> And when thou awakest, it shall talk with thee.
> —PROVERBS 6:22, KJV

Mornings are my best times of the day to hear from God, mostly because my mind hasn't had a chance to get burdened with all the day's problems and troubles. Now I am sure Elijah was not expecting the Lord to tell him the ravens would feed him. Ravens are scavengers; they are intelligent birds that will eat almost anything. But if God commands them not to touch meat good enough for human consumption, they won't. Child of God—get prepared to be fed by dirty birds. In these last days, God is going to command the greedy, wealthy ungodly to support His kingdom endeavors. Get ready— for the wealth of the wicked is stored up for the just.

Let's look at another example of God's Word leading and guiding His saints:

> Arise, get thee to Zarephath, which belongeth to
> Zidon, and dwell there: behold, I have commanded
> a widow woman to sustain thee.
> —1 KINGS 17:9, KJV

I am sure Elijah wasn't expecting to hear this: "go to Zidon and be sustained there." Zidon was a place of the Gentiles, and Gentiles were considered unclean; and besides that, he was told to "be sustained by a widow," a woman who had lost her husband, her means of support. Just think of how many times we've missed God's move because of exterior circumstances. Our job is to fill our minds and meditate upon God's Word, and God will lead and guide us.

Point B: "When thou sleepest, it shall keep thee."

This is very important. Reading and meditating on scripture before bed, keeps your dreams. The English word *keep* comes from the Hebrew word *shamar*, which means to "hedge," "guard," or "protect." When we sleep our minds go unprotected. That is why we say, "I can't help what I dream." This is when the devil tries to slip in and put fear and perversion and lies into our minds. Dreams affect us in different ways, good and bad. How many times have you had a dream that impacted you so much you thought about it for days or even weeks? That's the power of dreams, and that's why the devil wants access to them. Dreams take place in our imagination, our place of conception, and if God's Word is not there to protect them, the devil has free access to invade our dreams. We must be diligent about meditating on God's Word, as He told Joshua day and night. Let God's Word protect your imagination while you sleep so your dreams will be godly instead of demonic. I find it good to play the Bible on CD all through the night. You see, the spiritual part of us never sleeps, and our minds can be refreshed while our bodies rest. You would be surprised how much your physical being can benefit from God's living Word.

Look at what God's Word says about the effect His Word has on our physical body.

> It shall be health to thy navel, and marrow to thy bones.
>
> —PROVERBS 3:8, KJV

> For they are life unto those who find them, and health to all their flesh.
>
> —PROVERBS 4:22, KJV

> Pleasant words are as an honeycomb, sweet to the
> soul, and health to the bones.
> —PROVERBS 16:24, KJV

Filling your mind with the Word of God before sleep is so vital to us because God sometimes desires to speak to us through our dreams. The scriptures plainly tell that God's Word protects or guards what we dream at night. And that assures us that there will be no demonic influence in the dreams. And if it's a bad dream it could be a warning from God (as He monitors our dreams). It's also good to have a moment of listening when you first open your eyes, and if you remember your dream, ask the Lord for understanding. I've done that before and believe me; our God is faithful to answer. But what we should not do is open our eyes and immediately start thinking about the day's activities. Dedicate that time to the Lord. This leads into our final point.

Point C: "When thou wakest, it shall talk with thee."

I experience this everyday because of my meditation on the living Word. You see, in the morning when you awake, your mind is fresh and clear, free from all the activities the new day will bring. This is when I hear the living Word speak the clearest. When you first wake up in the morning, don't be in a hurry to think or speak. Try to keep your mind as clear as you can. This allows the living Word to speak to you. And if you had a godly dream because you meditated on the Word before you went to sleep, ask God to open up the meaning to you.

> I love them that love me; and those that seek me
> early shall find me.
> —PROVERBS 8:17, KJV

The way to hear God speak to you is to fill your mind with His Word and meditate on scripture. The scripture you're meditating on is not necessarily what God will say to you. That has happened to me many times. After biblical meditation, God said something way out in left field, and I found myself saying, "Where did that come from?" Only to find out it was something I needed for a later time.

> My son, keep thy father's commandment, and forsake not the law of thy mother: Bind them continually upon thine heart, and tie them about thy neck. When thou goest, it shall lead thee; when thou sleepest, it shall keep thee; and when thou awakest, it shall talk with thee.
>
> —PROVERBS 6:20–22, KJV

Let's take a look at the many blessings God promises His children for diligently feeding upon His living Word. We'll just look at the promises recorded in the Book of Proverbs.

God's Word shall:

> *Deliver you from the evil way of evil man, from the man that speaketh froward things (see Proverbs 2:12)*

> *Give you length of days and long life, and peace, shall they add to thee (see Proverbs 3:2).*

> *Help you find favor and good understanding in the sight of God and man (see Proverbs 3:4).*

> *Then shalt thou walk in thy way safely, and thy foot shall not stumble (see Proverbs 3:23).*

> *When thou liest down, thou shalt not be afraid: yea, thou shalt lie down, and thy sleep shall be sweet (see Proverbs 3:24).*

Forsake her not, and she shall preserve thee: love her and she shall keep thee (see Proverbs 4:6).

Exalt her, and she shall promote thee: she shall bring thee to honour, when thou dost embrace her (see Proverbs 4:8).

She shall give to thine head an ornament of grace: a crown of glory shall she deliver to thee (see Proverbs 4:9)

Hear, O my son, and receive my sayings: and the years of thy life shall be many (see Proverbs 4:10).

For they are life unto those that find them, and medicine to all their flesh (see Proverbs 4:22).

When thou goest, it shall lead you (see Proverbs 6:22).

When thou sleepest, it shall keep you (see Proverbs 6:22).

When thou awakest it shall talk to you (see Proverbs 6:22).

That they may keep thee from the strange women, from the stranger, which flattereth with her words (see Proverbs 7:5).

I wisdom dwell with prudence, and find out knowledge of witty inventions (see Proverbs 8:12).

That I may cause those that love me to inherit substance; and I will fill their treasures (see Proverbs 8:21).

This is the abundant life Jesus Christ died for us to have. He has given us all things that pertain unto life and godliness, through the knowledge of Him that hath called us to glory and virtue (see 2 Peter 1:3).

Child of God, the only way we're able to gain knowledge of our God is through His living Word, Jesus Christ.

> That which was from the beginning, which we have heard, which we have seen with our eyes, which we have looked upon, and our hands have handled, of the Word of life.
>
> —1 JOHN 1:1, KJV

The disciple John declares, "We heard the Word speak; we saw the Word with our own eyes; we handled the Word with our own hands." Now the church can declare: "We fellowship with the living Word inside our hearts, within our imaginations."

Chapter 10

IMAGINE GOD

THE BIBLE ENCOURAGES us to use our imagination in many ways. The Bible is full of metaphors and parables designed to stir our imagination. King David understood this very well. Let's start by looking at Psalm 121:1:

> I will lift up mine eyes unto the hills, from whence
> cometh my help (KJV).

David was not talking about physical hills where God was present. He's talking about lifting up his inner eyes within his imagination and gazing at the promises written in his heart. This is what the apostle James is talking about in James 1:21:

> Receive with meekness the engrafted Word, which
> is able to save your souls (KJV).

When God's Word is engrafted or written in your heart, it's there for good, and no devil in hell can remove it. This happens because you've meditated or memorized scripture to the point it becomes part of you.

When something is written or engrafted, you can see it, and because it's living or alive, it's able to speak as well as show you visions and dreams. As a matter of fact, God's Word written in your thoughts can do anything or become anything He chooses because He is God. He told Moses, "I am that I am." In other words, "Son, if you let Me in I can become whoever or whatever you need Me to be or become!" James tells us that the engrafted Word is able to save your souls. David knew where his help came from; it came from inside his own heart. That's where he looked. That's where he found the living Word, and His name is Jesus!

> But mine eyes are unto thee O GOD the Lord, in
> thee is my trust; leave not my soul destitute.
> —PSALM 141:8, KJV

David could not physically see the Lord, but he could "see" Him though God's Word to his imagination.

> My voice shalt thou hear in the morning, O Lord.
> in the morning will I direct my prayer unto thee,
> and will look up.
> —PSALM 5:3, KJV

David was not looking for God with his natural eyes, but with his inner eyes of his imagination. Because of David's great love for God's Word, surely he saw or heard from God inside.

> I will stand upon my watch, and set me upon the
> tower, and will watch to see what he will say unto
> me, and what I shall answer when I am reproved.
> —HABAKKUK 2:1, KJV

The prophet is going to his place of prayer to pray to the Lord and look for signs or words within his imagination. Notice he says, "I will watch to see what He will say unto me." Visions within our imagination may come to us in images or words.

> Consider and hear me, O LORD my God: lighten
> mine eyes, lest I sleep the sleep of death.
> —PSALM 13:3, KJV

Here we have King David crying out to God to "lighten my eyes." The king knew his very life depended on wisdom, revelation, and vision from God. God deposits these things in our imagination, the place where thoughts, plans, and ideas form, the place of conception.

God placed parables and metaphors throughout the Bible to stir our imaginations. The Bible teaches us to imagine God as our Father.

> Our Father which are in heaven, Hallowed be thy name.
> —MATTHEW 6:9, KJV

> But thou, when thou prayest, enter into thy closet, and when thou hast shut thy door, pray to thy Father which is in secret; and thy Father which seeth in secret shall reward thee openly.
> —MATTHEW 6:6, KJV

> If ye then, being evil, know how to give good gifts unto your children, how much more shall your Father which is in heaven give good things to them that ask him?
> —MATTHEW 7:11, KJV

Imagining God to be our Father can give us a sense of security. The Father is the protector, the provider, and the disciplinarian. Seeing God as our Father also gives us feelings of family, love, and relationship. This brings God close to us and gives us hope.

The Bible also teaches us to imagine God as *fire*.

> For our God is a consuming fire.
> —HEBREWS 12:29, KJV

Imagining God as fire helps us to understand God can comfort us as a fire on a cold night. And as fire, God can also give us light to help us find our way when we're lost. It also helps us understand that like fire, God can destroy our enemy before our very eyes (like a consuming fire).

The Bible instructs us to imagine God as our *rock, fortress, buckler, high tower*:

> The LORD is my rock, and my fortress, and my deliverer; my God, my strength, in whom I will trust; my buckler, and the horn of my salvation, and my high tower.
>
> —PSALM 18:2, KJV

Shield

> The LORD is my strength and my shield; my heart trusted in him, and I am helped: therefore my heart greatly rejoiceth; and with my song will I praise him.
>
> —PSALM 28:7, KJV

Light

> The LORD is my light and my salvation; whom shall I fear? the LORD is the strength of my life; of whom shall I be afraid?
>
> —PSALM 27:1, KJV

Lion

> And one of the elders saith unto me, Weep not: behold, the Lion of the tribe of Judah, the Root of David, hath prevailed to open the book, and to loose the seven seals thereof.
>
> —REVELATION 5:5, KJV

Lamb

And I beheld, and, lo, in the midst of the throne
and of the four beasts, and in the midst of the
elders, stood a Lamb as it had been slain, having
seven horns and seven eyes, which are the seven
Spirits of God sent forth into all the earth.

—REVELATION 5:6, KJV

Bright Morning Star

I Jesus have sent mine angel to testify unto you
these things in the churches. I am the root and the
offspring of David, and the bright and morning
star.

—REVELATION 22:16, KJV

Rose of Sharon, Lily of the Valleys

I am the rose of Sharon, and the lily of the
valleys.

—SONG OF SOLOMON 2:1, KJV

Living Water

He that believeth on me, as the scripture hath said,
out of his belly shall flow rivers of living water.

—JOHN 7:38, KJV

Bread of Life

And Jesus said unto them, I am the bread of life:
he that cometh to me shall never hunger; and he
that believeth on me shall never thirst.

—JOHN 6:35, KJV

King of Kings

> And he hath on his vesture and on his thigh a name written, KING OF KINGS, AND LORD OF LORDS.
>
> —REVELATION 19:16, KJV

High Tower

> My goodness, and my fortress; *my high tower*, and my deliverer; my shield, and he in whom I trust; who subdueth my people under me.
>
> —PSALM 144:2, KJV, EMPHASIS ADDED

Rushing Mighty Wind

> And suddenly there came a sound from heaven as of a *rushing mighty wind*, and it filled all the where they were sitting.
>
> —ACTS 2:2, EMPHASIS ADDED

Rain

> Then shall we know, if we follow on to know the LORD: his going forth is prepared as the morning; and he shall come unto us as the rain, as the latter and former rain unto the earth.
>
> —HOSEA 6:3, KJV

Captain of the Lord's Host

> And the captain of the LORD's host said unto Joshua, Loose thy shoe from off thy foot; for the place whereon thou standest is holy. And Joshua did so.
>
> —JOSHUA 5:15, KJV

Each one of these metaphors depicts some of the characteristics of our Great God, while they also give us comfort in knowing He's our Heavenly Father. Let's fill our minds with God's Word and meditate on it daily. As His Word sinks deep into our imagination, we will begin to imagine God. And as we imagine God by meditating on His Living Word, we will begin to see ourselves as He sees us; we will begin to be led by the Holy Spirit. We will see things to come, as well as know the hope of His calling. God's Word is forever established in heaven, and all power in heaven and Earth backs it up. We should be eternally grateful to our God for allowing us to possess this great treasure. Remember, to imagine God is to allow His Word into your imagination by meditation.

Chapter 11

WE NEED DISCERNMENT

As we discussed, the devil has access to our minds because of man's fall in the Garden of Eden. That knowledge of evil that we all were born with belongs to the devil. Therefore, since it's his, he has a right to come into your mind and try to get you to use that knowledge. Satan has no authority over us, just access to our minds, and he comes to steal, kill, and destroy. There are three voices we must learn to discern: the voice of our spirit, the voice of God, and the voice of the devil. Let's take a look at John 10:1–2:

> Verily, verily, I say unto you, He that entereth not by the door into the sheepfold, but climbeth up some other way, the same is a thief and a robber (KJV).

In this scripture, the sheepfold is this world and the door is the birth canal. Jesus is telling us whosoever came through the door is the Good Shepherd, and the door is the legal entry to this world. Now we know Jesus was born of a woman, so he came into this world legally. God does not and will not break His laws. Notice the thief climbed in some other way; this tells us the devil is an illegal alien and was under Adam's God-given authority, but as you know that authority was forfeited in the Garden of Eden. Let's look at John 10:3:

> To him the porter openeth; and the sheep hear his voice; and He calleth his own sheep by name, and leadeth them out (KJV).

The porter is your spirit-man, and if you're born again your spirit-man will always open the gate to the voice of the Lord. Now, the problem within Christianity today is we are distracted from hearing the voice of the Shepherd clearly because of the cares of this world, persecution, the deceitfulness of riches, tribulation, stress, anxiety, doubt, and diverse fears. All of those worldly problems crowd our minds and block the still small voice of the Shepherd. Now, the question is, are we His sheep? Jesus said, "My sheep hear my voice and follow me." I personally believe that we need to be taught how to hear the Shepherd's voice, and we're covering a lot of that in this book. As we have gone over already, God's Word dwelling in your heart is the first step to hearing and knowing the voice of the Shepherd.

> For the word of God *is* living and powerful, and sharper than any two-edged sword, piercing even to the division of soul and spirit, and of joints and marrow, and is a discerner of the thoughts and intents of the heart.
>
> —HEBREWS 4:12, KJV

The word *discerner* comes from the Greek word *kriteekos,* which means a judge (a critical judge). Filling your mind with God's Word will alert you to that alien voice that comes to kill, steal, and destroy. Then you have to take the responsibility and cast those demonic thoughts down by not agreeing with them and not accepting them. You see, what the devil is trying to do is get you to agree with his evil scheme that will lead you astray from the voice of the Shepherd.

> For though by this time you ought to be teachers, you need *someone* to teach you again the first principles of the oracles of God; and you have come to need milk and not solid food. For everyone who partakes *only* of milk *is* unskilled in the word

of righteousness, for he is a babe. But solid food
belongs to those who are of full age, *that is,* those
who by reason of use have their senses exercised to
discern both good and evil.

—Hebrews 5:12–14, kjv

Not long ago as I pondered on the condition of the church, the
Lord gave me a vision. In this vision I saw a gigantic man standing
on the Earth. The vision started from his head and went down to
the ground. His face was the face of a very old man; his hair and
beard were long and white. And then I noticed that he had no cloth-
ing over his torso and the hair on his chest was white as well. Then
the vision moved down to his abdomen and there I was shocked,
because this very old man was wearing a diaper. Then I heard the
Lord say, "This is the church!" Look at the end of the text mentioned
above: "those, who by reason of use, have their senses exercised to
discern both good and evil" (Heb. 5:14). Paul is telling us to put the
Word of God to use. How do we put the Word to use? We do this by
speaking it, meditating on it, obeying it, and living it. This strength-
ens our senses or perception, which means we can now distinguish
or recognize which voice is God's and which voice is Satan's. Have
you ever had someone tell you a lie, and somehow you just knew
it was a lie? Have you ever had someone offer you a proposal, and
you just knew it was not a good one even though on the outside
it looked good? Have you ever been driving and gotten lost, but
somehow you knew which way to turn? God's Word will increase
our perception in both physical and spiritual realms if we give Him
a chance. This discernment is what young Solomon asked God for,
and it pleased the Lord that he asked for discernment above riches
and honor and preeminence. Solomon understood the importance
of the ability to discern good from evil in both realms. He earnestly
prayed and asked God for what we have at our disposal and rarely
use, the Word of God.

Spiritual discernment is something that we must continue to seek.

It should be our daily bread, for the Word of God is our daily bread. Let's take a look into King David's life—a man after God's own heart, and a man who yearned for the Word of the Living God.

> And Satan stood up against Israel, and provoked David to number Israel.
> —1 CHRONICLES 21:1, KJV

Notice when Satan takes a stand against a nation, he goes after the leadership. He uses the same tactic with the church; he goes after the leaders. The Bible says he "provoked" or "enticed" King David to sin against the God he loved. This manipulation took place in David's imagination, within his thoughts. David's discernment must have been weak at this point of his life because I find it hard to believe this man would knowingly risk the lives of thousands of people. The devil watches and waits for the right opportunity to move in and attack, for he knows when we have been slack concerning God's Word. The Devil probably personalized thoughts to David's mind to make him believe it was his idea to number the people. He uses this disguise to deceive us into doing his will. Because of David's sin, seventy thousand men died at the hand of the Lord. Do you see the need for discernment? Well, it's at your disposal all the time!

Chapter 12

THE HIDDEN MAN OF THE HEART

I COULD NOT CONTINUE writing this book without a teaching on a very important person, *the new you!* So far, we've been examining our thoughts, imagination, emotions, and will, which make up the soul of mankind or what the Bible sometimes calls "the heart." But now, we should take a look at the perfected part of every born-again believer, the spirit-man. There has been a lot of confusion about the three dimensions of man, but after twenty years of dedicated study it's becoming clearer and clearer to me. An easy indication that God is speaking to us about our *spirit-man* is He calls it a *man*. Never is the heart, soul, or mind depicted as an individual or person. Man is a spirit that possesses a soul, and temporally lives in a body. We are made in the image of God, who the Bible teaches is a Spirit. When Adam and Eve fell in the Garden, they died spiritually, and this happened immediately, but they lived physically for hundreds of years after they fell (remember, death means separation). They were spiritually disconnected from God, and that condition has been passed down to all mankind. Therefore, we must be born again (meaning spiritually connected again with our heavenly Father) to see the kingdom of God. Let's see what God's Word says about our spirit-man.

> But he that is joined unto the Lord is one spirit.
> —1 CORINTHIANS 6:17, KJV

Upon conversion, we are joined to the Holy Ghost, and the word *joined* is taken from the Greek word *kollao*, which means to "glue" or to "cleave." This scripture goes on to say that when this cleaving takes place, we become one spirit with the Lord. God in all His splendor and perfection is unified with our human spirit giving God a place inside man to fellowship along with the Word. Now we have Jesus Christ the Word dwelling in us, as well as the Holy Spirit. This is so wonderfully explained by our Lord in John 14:23:

> If a man love me, he will keep my words: and my
> Father will love him, and we will come unto him,
> and make our abode with him (KJV).

What a wonderful truth this is. Jesus is telling us that He and the Father will make their abode with those who love Him and obey Him. Now we've learned that the Spirit of the Father cleaves to our spirit-man and we become born again, but where does our spirit-man abide? We know from our prior studies that the Word comes to abide within our heart and our imagination. Now where is our spirit-man located? In 1 Peter 3:4, Peter tells us, "But let it be the hidden man of the heart, in that which is not corruptible" (KJV). Our born-again spirit-man is strengthened as God's Holy Spirit cleaves to it, and they both dwell alongside Christ the Word in our heart and imagination. They all walk upon the soil of our mind in the midst of our thoughts and imaginations.

> For this cause I bow my knees unto the Father of
> our Lord Jesus Christ, Of whom the whole family
> in heaven and earth is named, That he would grant
> you, according to the riches of his glory, to be
> strengthened with might by his Spirit in the inner
> man; That Christ may dwell in your hearts by faith;
> that ye, being rooted and grounded in love.
> —EPHESIANS 3:14–17, KJV

You may wonder why they dwell amongst our thoughts and imagination. They dwell there to help make our thoughts and imaginations rooted and planted in the soil of love. Why not go to the problem area of man? This is where we need all the help we can get. Let's go to the book of wisdom that reaches throughout all time and dispensations.

> The spirit of man is the candle of the LORD, searching all the inward parts of the belly.
> —PROVERBS 20:27, KJV

Our spirit-man is now light in the Lord, and it searches through our thoughts and imagination. Now that our spirits are re-connected to the Father, they assist the Lord in judging our thoughts and intentions, and they bring revelation to our minds.

> For ye were sometimes darkness, but now are ye light in the Lord: walk as children of light.
> —EPHESIANS 5:8, KJV

I think it's amazing how our God reestablished unity with those who love Him by joining His precious Holy Spirit with our darkened human spirit, creating a new creation in Christ Jesus. The only thing good in us is God, and because of His sinless nature, He could not dwell within our sinful minds, but He can dwell within Himself within our minds. So our born-again spirits play a big part in the renewing of our minds because they contain the nature of God within an unrenewed mind. Because God is in our newly created spirits, it is impossible for us to sin spiritually. Look at what the apostle John tells us:

> Whosoever is born of God doth not commit sin; for his seed remaineth in him: and he cannot sin, because he is born of God.
> —1 JOHN 3:9, KJV

This scripture has been difficult for us to understand because we've been looking at it wrong. Yes, we have all sinned and come short of the glory of God and we are yet sinning, but that's according to our flesh, not our spirits. What John is saying is that it is impossible for a born-again spirit to sin because God's divine nature fills a child of God's Spirit. Listen, that's the real you, that part of you just waiting on the perfected mind to manifest. Then we will be like Jesus! Listen to Paul in his frustration:

> For I delight in the law of God after the inward man: But I see another law in my members, warring against the law of my mind, and bringing me into captivity to the law of sin which is in my members.
>
> —ROMANS 7:22–23, KJV

Paul admits that his spirit-man has no problem with sin; it's the struggle of the unrenewed mind and the flesh that causes him to fall. Let's look at 1 John 4:17:

> Herein is our love made perfect, that we may have boldness in the day of judgment: because as He is, so are we in this world (KJV).

God loves us, so He had to have a holy place within us to commune, and that's our born-again spirits. This verse tells us, as He is now pure and holy, blameless and righteous, so are we—right now in this evil world. But only in our spirits are we made the righteousness of God in Christ Jesus, until our change comes.

> The secret things belong to the LORD our God, but those things which are revealed belong to us and to our children forever, that we may do all the words of this law.
>
> —DEUTERONOMY 29:29, NKJV

This verse tells us that revelation is given to us by God to help us obey all the Word of God. Revelation from God's Word gives us the application of the Word.

Chapter 13

THE EYES OF THE LORD

I will instruct you and teach you in the way you
should go; I will guide you with My eye.

PSALM 32:8, NKJV

HERE WE HAVE David receiving a clear word concerning how God desires to instruct and teach David the things He wants him to know. He says, "I will guide you with my eye." Now the Word of God is very consistent, and there is no discrepancy in it at all. What's happening here is God using a metaphor to make a spiritual truth plain to us all. The eye represents vision, sight, and the ability to see. God is making a comparison between His eyes and His Word, and the message to us is that as important as our physical eyes are for seeing where we're going, God has designed His Word to lead us supernaturally through the natural realm and the spiritual realm. Remember Paul tells us that we see through a mirror dimly, meaning we need help with our spiritual perception. But our heavenly Father loves us, so He's given us His Word to lead and guide us. Let's look at another example of the Lord's eyes and His Word:

The eyes of the LORD preserve knowledge, and he overthroweth the words of the transgressor.

—PROVERBS 22:12, KJV

Here it is again, the eyes of the Lord being compared to the Word of the Lord. The Word instructs us, teaches us, guides us, and preserves knowledge for us. These scriptures show us that to see through the eyes of the Lord, we must see through the Living Word. When we see things through His eyes, the first thing we clearly understand is God is in total control over every situation and circumstance. Then comes the realization that with God all things are possible. Let's look at James 1:23–25:

> For if any be a hearer of the word, and not a doer,
> he is like unto a man beholding his natural face
> in a glass: For he beholdeth himself, and goeth his
> way, and straightway forgetteth what manner of
> man he was. But whoso looketh into the perfect
> law of liberty, and continueth therein, he being not
> a forgetful hearer, but a doer of the work, this man
> shall be blessed in his deed (KJV).

We've already established that looking through the eyes of the Lord is looking into His Word by way of meditation. But notice what happens when we look into the Word; we see ourselves as God sees us, victorious, prosperous, overcomers. But notice the first man goes on his way after looking into the mirror and forgets who he is in Christ. It's so important that we meditate on who God says we are, we must not forget because that's our victory. Now notice that the second man who looks into the mirror of God's Word continues therein. He's blessed because of his communion with the living Word, meaning he goes over what he's heard over and over until it sticks; just as in Joshua 1:8, he is blessed in his deed. I don't know about you, but I want to prosper in all that I do. I want to have good success. I want to be like a tree, planted by the rivers of water-bearing fruit in my season, and I want to be blessed in my deeds. Let's make a conscious decision to ponder, to meditate, to continue in God's Word day and night and watch what God will do!

> But we all, with unveiled face, beholding as in a
> mirror the glory of the Lord, are being transformed
> into the same image from glory to glory, just as by
> the Spirit of the Lord.
>
> —2 Corinthians 3:18, nkjv

As we look into God's Word, we see the glory of the Lord revealed in our lives. And this is important for us to realize, because Satan's lies can sometimes cause us to doubt who we are in Christ if we allow them to. But God's mirror will reveal the truth to us, and it's the truth that makes us free. Seeing ourselves as God sees us causes a transformation to take place deep within our hearts. This liberty is given to us by the Spirit of Truth, or as we learned earlier, the Spirit of the Word.

God gave us words to describe this physical world we live in, and we have been given the ability to see the world with our physical eyes and with our spiritual eyes in our imagination. If natural words describe physical objects, God's supernatural Word describes beyond the physical realm and if we allow it, the Word will show us unseen things to the natural eyes for the purposes of God. Unseen things are shown to us to give us hope in times of trouble. Have you ever been in a bad situation where it seemed like there was no way out, and you opened up the Bible and your eyes just happened to lock on a certain passage of scripture that spoke hope to you and you were comforted by that hope? You held on to that verse with everything within you until you began to see God in the midst of the storm. And when you saw God's hand at work, you found peace beyond your own understanding because you suddenly realized all things work together for your good. Then you saw yourself out of it in your imagination, or you saw yourself out of it by a strong inner witness; either way God gets the glory because through His Word you were able to see unseen things. God sees the end from the beginning, meaning He sees the end result. He saw me as a man of God when I was struggling with addiction. Therefore, He granted me mercy to make it through those dark days. God has the ability to look at the solution instead of the problem, and that's what His Word will allow us to do when we meditate on it.

> For thus says the High and Lofty One Who inhabits eternity, whose name is Holy: "I dwell in the high and holy place, With him who has a contrite and humble spirit, To revive the spirit of the humble, And to revive the heart of the contrite ones."
> —ISAIAH 57:15, NKJV

God rules eternity, meaning He rules all past, all present, and all the future. But notice what the Almighty is saying, "I dwell in eternity with the humble ones." Now, let's look at Ecclesiastes 3:11:

> He has made everything beautiful in its time. Also He has put eternity in their hearts, except that no one can find out the work that God does from beginning to end (NKJV).

I believe this eternity in us is one of the many meeting places with God within our hearts. This scripture tells us even though eternity dwells within us, we only have the revelation God allows us to have.

> Eye has not seen, nor ear heard, Nor have entered into the heart of man the things which God has prepared for those who love Him. But God has revealed them to us through His Spirit.
> —1 CORINTHIANS 2:9–10, NKJV

Our imagination is placed in this eternal part of our heart. I say this because it's the part of our mind that reaches out into our future. Our memory holds our past, and our imagination holds our future, which makes our imagination prophetic. The way we see ourselves doing things we haven't done is through our imagination. And it's there God shows us who we are and who we will become through His living Word. God's Word within our imagination becomes a compass for our future.

> Where there is no vision, the people perish.
> —PROVERBS 29:18, KJV

The Word of God is our vision because it speaks God's perfect will for all things, and it speaks *logos* and *rhema*. Look at 2 Chronicles 32:32:

> Now the rest of the acts of Hezekiah, and his goodness, behold, they are written in the vision of Isaiah the prophet, the son of Amoz, and in the book of the kings of Judah and Israel (KJV).

Here we have God's written Word referred to as the vision of Isaiah instead of the Book of Isaiah. So what Proverbs 29:18 is saying, is where there is no revelation from God's Word, the people perish.

> The secret things belong to the LORD our God,
> but those things, which are revealed belong to us
> and to our children forever, that we may do all
> the words of this law.
> —DEUTERONOMY 29:29, NKJV

This verse tells us that revelation is given by God to us to help us obey all the Word of God.

> I have more understanding than all my teachers,
> for Your testimonies are my meditation.
> —PSALM 119:99, NKJV

> Oh, how I love Your law! It is my meditation all
> the day.
> —PSALM 119:97, NKJV

I find it amazing that as busy as King David was, running that great nation, he found time to meditate on God's Word all day long. This shows us David knew the wonderful benefits of meditating on the Word, and it takes away our excuses about being too busy to think on the Word during our workday. Listen, just pray and find a new verse every day, and keep it in your mind. Every opportunity that arises, go back to, and watch the results you get!

TO CONTACT THE AUTHOR

efearman@yahoo.com